MY WALK WITH

FAITH

THROUGH THE WILDERNESS

"A test of faith"

DR. WILLIE E. CLEVELAND

WESTBOW
PRESS®
A DIVISION OF THOMAS NELSON
& ZONDERVAN

WestBow Press books may be ordered through booksellers or by contacting:

WestBow Press
A Division of Thomas Nelson & Zondervan
1663 Liberty Drive
Bloomington, IN 47403
www.westbowpress.com
1 (866) 928-1240

ISBN: 978-1-5127-3240-5 (sc)

Library of Congress Control Number: 2016902972

Print information available on the last page.

WestBow Press rev. date: 03/02/2016

Contents

Tribute to My Wife Mary

I Give Your Flowers

I honor you for thirty-nine years as my wife and mother of our six children. I salute you for being my sister in Christ for the last thirty three years. I offer you your flowers while you can smell them, for your serving under my leadership. I

You have served as the spiritual mother of your Galatain family and leader of women ministry for twenty-three years.

Whenever I celebrate my pastoral anniversary, I always reflect back to each year you were there supporting me. Every time I tell the story of my test of faith, my journey through the wilderness, I always give honor to my Lord who brought us through the wilderness.

Yet, I find it difficult if not impossible, to tell my story without acknowledging that you were the constant, tangible one who was there for me. You were the one I had to lean on during the difficult and stressful times. As strong as I may have been physically, you were as strong spiritually. As weary at times as I may have been trying to get to the finish line, I do not believe I would have made it without you by my side. Truly, it was your constant cheering me on, as a cheerleader cheers for her special player. Your cheering encouraged me to keep pressing toward goal.

We have been back for thirteen years, and you are still my strongest cheerleader and support. I thank our Lord for your love and commitment. I never played organization sports, but I have been told that sometimes having the home crowd cheering for their team can make a difference.

You made the greatest difference, second to our Lord and god Jesus Christ. Mary, your leadership reminds me of the prophetess Deborah, the wife of Lapidoth, one of Israel's judges. She led Israel in battle just as you have lead the women of Galatian. I thank the Lord for giving me you not to be my better half but my other half.

To My Galatian
Missionary Baptist Church Family
Straight from the Heart

I believe it was the gospel singer Andre Crouch who penned these words to a song, "How can I forget all the things you done for me?" Of course I believe that he was expressing his gratitude to the Lord. Many times, I have thanked our Lord for leading us through some very difficult times. I am still thanking the Lord for every one of you who followed my leadership through the wilderness journey.

I am sure that there were times on our journey that some of you may have doubts as to whether we would ever make it back home. Some, if not all of you became discouraged at times, yet you hung in there and stayed the course with me.

I cannot begin to express how much I appreciate you for not grumbling and complaining every time we had to move to another location. We started our on our journey with approximately one hundred members who were not afraid to follow me. I thank the Lord that the day when we returned home, it was with the same one hundred members who were not afraid plus few more added to the fold. I dare not try to name every one of the one hundred for fear of missing someone's name. I thank every minister, deacon, and trustee, ministry leader, and members who supported me through our journey. Finally, every times I informed you that we had to move, it was a test of faith. For me, it was a confirmation that the Lord was with us. I believe that the Lord was showing me through your confidence in me that you believed the Lord was with me. You believed that the Lord was leading and guiding me as I led you through the wilderness.

My Supporting Cast

There are three sisters and one brother in Christ who played a very important part in the development of my book. They are Gurtha Smith, Frances McCowian, Sheila

Hunt Thomas and Stanley Sergeant. I called them my four friends because they have proven themselves to be friends and my supporting cast.

At the infancy of the book, my good friend and sister in Christ Gurtha, labored as she started the typing process of my manuscript. I joked that my penmanship is much like some doctor's-hard to read but Gurtha took on the enormous task of converting my words from my handwritten notes to a typed copy.

Frances, who is one of my spiritual daughters, intercepted the process from Gurtha's typed version. Frances devoted much time and patience as she put my story into print via computer. Her talent and creativity started the transformation into a book. Later my publisher and editor completed the process.

My close friend and sister in Christ, Sheila, played the role of supporting cast, by critiquing every word. I wanted the manuscript to be as error free as possible before I presented it to my publisher. Both Sheila and Frances offered their love and words of encouragement, which helped to inspire me to complete my manuscript. It was important to complete my manuscript. Having family and friends who believed in my vision to writer my book gave me the determination to finish my book. I will always be grateful to my supporting cast for their willingness to help me.

Finally, Stanley is more like a son than a nephew and yet he is also a brother in Christ. Stan helped me with the collection of pictures that I used to help illustrate my wilderness experience. His audio-visual and computer skills have been a great help to me and I am appreciative of his support.

(A special appreciation)

There are so many people I could thank for their words of encouragement during my journey but spaces and time will not allow me to name them all. There is one special brother in Christ who offered his support at a critical time during my journey, his name is James Henry.

James Henry is the proprietor of the C.W. Morris/ James Henry home for funerals in Highland Park, Michigan. From my Pastor's perspective, it is more than just a funeral home. He and his staff are a Christian family that offers sincere comfort and support to those who are grieving.

James Henry is a Christian brother who is always considerate of the financial struggles or difficulties of any family that may not have burial insurance. Those who have insurance and regardless of the amount he always makes it clear they have several choices. Whenever one of my Galatian family members or my biological family member makes his or her transition, I always recommend or call James Henry.

In September 1994 after Galatian experienced the fire, I received a call from James Henry. He explained to me that he had heard about the fire. He told me that he knew we were looking for a building to have worship service and

Bible study. He offered his prays and his support in anyway he could be of help.

Before the conversation ended James Henry told me that he has two chapels in his home for funerals. He told me that I could use the smaller chapel during the week for Bible study and the large chapel on Sunday Morning for worship.

He also told me that we didn't have to pay any rent and that we could use the chapels for as long as we needed to. I was overwhelmed with joy and appreciation to know that he cared enough about me and my Galatian family to extend his home for funerals to us.

I presented the offer to my Galatian family and asked them to take it under consideration. After considering the offer, for various reasons, we decided that we would look for another building and location. There are some professed Christians who are not comfortable worshipping in funeral homes and so we kept looking, although one day we all will need the service of a home for funerals director.

I will always be grateful to James Henry who proved himself to be a friend indeed when we were in need. After thirteen years of being home, he and I still have a very close relationship as he continues to serve my Galatian family and biological family.

Introduction

When I was a young boy, I learned through my mother's battle with tuberculosis why having a strong faith in Christ is so important. During the late 1950s, my mother was admitted to Herman Kiefer Hospital in Detroit, Michigan where she stayed as patient for one year.

Tuberculosis was as fatal back in the 50's, 60's as some cancers are today. Yes my father, sibling and I feared because it was a very serious disease. Doctors did not have the medical knowledge then to treat many medical conditions as they do today. Thank the Lord God for bestowing mankind with the wisdom and that has advanced medical technology. It is my belief that God performs healings through  doctors who prescribe healing medicines, and through different types of surgeries that helps to repaired and restored us. Nevertheless I believe by faith God still performs the miraculous through various methods. When I pray for someone's healing, I say "Lord whatever way you choose to heal, your will be done."

Can you imagine how scared we were as kids to know that our mother was gravely sick? There were times when we weren't sure if mother would recover and come home to us. We would go to the hospital to see her but were not allowed to visit her room. I think it was because she had to be isolated and hospital rules were very strict. We had to stand outside the window of her room on ground level and wave to her as she looked out the window and wave to us. My father and mother's faith in the power of prayer never seemed to waver; even in the midst of what we were told was a life-threatening illness.

As a young boy, although I didn't completely understand how my parents' faith was being tested, my siblings and I rode on their faith. We were still learning and developing our faith in Jesus Christ. (You see it is our personal experiencing of the power of God that develops our faith). We witnessed our mother's full recovery from Tuberculosis and watched her live the rest of her life for Christ. She served Him faithfully until her battle with dementia prevented her from coming to Church. After approximately ten years battling against dementia she finally made her transition in April 2007. Paul's words gave my family and I comfort II Corinthians 5:8-9 *8We are confident, I say, and willing rather to be absent from the body, and to be present with the Lord 9Wherefore we labor, that whether present or absent, we may be accepted of Him.*

While still a young boy I accept Jesus Christ as my Savor and began to lean on my parents understanding about the Lord until I became spiritually mature. I have heard parents say "I am not going to choose a religion for my child, he or she can choose for themselves when they are old enough. That is very dangerous position for a parent take, considering that there are so many none Christian cults seeking out the young and the innocent. My parent decision to introduce us to Christ put all eleven Cleveland children on the right path and connected us with the true Lord and savior.

I matured or grew spiritually from a young boy into a Christian man. I grew from a lay member of the Church into serving in many capacities and became a minister of the Gospel of Jesus Christ. My spiritual growth leads me to believe that I had two strong Christian characteristics or fruit of the Spirit, which are faith and patience. It was easy then to say I have faith when all was well and there weren't any adversities in my life. It was easy to say I have faith that can move mountains—until the adversary put a mountain into my path (Metaphorically)

I used to sing a gospel song recorded by the late Rev. James Cleveland (possibly related) the title If you have the faith" James Cleveland declares, If you have the faith to believe, you can say to the mountain, mountain I want you to move." But I didn't fully understand that singing words about faith doesn't mean that I have faith or that my faith was strong and unwavering.

I also learned that the mountain Jesus talked about was a figurative mountain that represents the different obstacles and stumbling blocks that we born-gain believers in Christ Jesus face while on this Christian journey. Matthew 21:21 *21Jesus replied, truly I tell you, if you have faith and do not doubt, not only can you do what was done to the fig tree, but also you can say to this mountain, 'Go, throw yourself into the sea, and it will be done.*

It was Jesus who spoke these words to His disciples in John 15:18-19 *18If the world hates you, keep in mind that it hated Me first 19If you belong to the world, it would love you as its own. As it is, you do not belong to the world, but I have chosen you out of the world. That is why the world hates you.*

Here Jesus was talking to His disciples and to us today who have come to know Him as Lord and savior of our lives. Christians must understand that because we are still in the world, we are not exempt from the troubles, trials, and tribulations of the world. As long as we are the world there will always be mountains in our path.

Unfortunately there are some who teach that we should not have any problems, if you have faith. Jesus told His disciples "If the world hates Me your Master, how much more will they hate you My servants?" His words surely apply to Christians today and I believe that Jesus' words are the final authority.

The Bible teaches us that there are two kinds of faith and two kinds of test in which believers in Christ must learn to discern:

1. There is the saving faith that man believes unto righteousness and salvation (Romans 10:9-10 *⁹That if you declare with your mouth, Jesus is Lord," and believe in your heart that God has raised Him from the dead, you will be saved ¹⁰For it is with your heart that you believe and are justified, and it is with your and with your mouth that you profess your faith and are saved."*

2. There is an inward faith that allows Christians to spiritually see through the (metaphorical) mountain that may be in their path and view the divine attributes of God.

Matthew 15:21–28, the Canaanite woman's faith in Jesus Christ was unwavering. She looked beyond her figurative mountain, which was the condition of her demon-possessed daughter and saw the healing power of Jesus.

It was easy to say, "I have faith" when all was well and there weren't any adversities in my life. It was easy to say, "I have faith that can move mountains"—until the Adversary put a mountain in my path.

Trials and Tests

My brethren, count it all joy when ye fall
into divers temptations.

—James 1:2

There is an old saying, "God bless the child who has his own." Faith's tests or trials comes in many ways and forms but what I believe is most important, will you be able to stand the test? The more rooted and grounded believers are in the word of God the more strength we will have to stand during the test. There is truth to the statement "No test, no testimony" I wouldn't be in the position to give my testimony, had it not been for the test. This book is a testimony of God's power and my faith.

In 1977 the month of June my wife, children, and I lost our home due to hard times and poor stewardship. We didn't have anywhere to go but I believe that the Lord touched the heart of one of my siblings, and we moved in with him and his family. If you don't have a personal relationship with Christ, it is hard to find joy when you are homeless. Several months later, we had to move in with my wife's grandmother, but I never lost hope in finding our own home one day. Finally, in February 1978, at the beginning of the month, we moved into our new home. Faith. We prayed about our living condition while homeless but I understood that prayer without works was dead. It is my belief that there are some prayers

1

that require works. I call it "What are you doing to help your prayer" also believe that the Lord expect us to some things that we can and should do to help ourselves. While we were homeless, I worked two fulltime jobs to earn enough money for a down payment on house. It was faith in action and not prayer waiting for God to act on our behalf. It was my understanding that the Lord made it possible for to obtain two jobs which produced the income we needed to buy another house.

We use to sing a song titled "One step" It goes like this, One, one step, all I have to do is take one step and He (The Lord) will do the rest. I did my part by working and the Lord did bless us with enough to buy a house through an unconventional method at that time. Bad credit foreclosure in our financial history. Although we had bad credit we were able assumed a mortgage. It truly was a test of our faith as well as our resolve to not faint during the test.

> *³Because you know that the testing of your faith produces patience ⁴let perseverance have finish it work so that you may be mature and complete, not lacking anything.*
>
> —James 1:3–4

This word *temptation* means "tests or trials." God allows believers to be tested and to go through trials, whereas the second kind of test is a temptation of the devil.

> *When tempted by evil, no one should say, God is tempting me, nor does He tempt anyone.*
>
> —James 1:13

Then was Jesus led up of the Spirit into the wilderness, to be tempted of the devil.

—Matthew 4:1

It is important for believers in Christ Jesus to know that God does allow us to be tested through or by the trials of life, but God does not tempt us with evil. God was not responsible for our homelessness because I made some unwise financial decisions. God didn't put us to a test nor did God tempt us with evil. But we suffered the consequences from some unwise or bad decisions. I didn't blame God but I did pray asking Him to fix up my mess up.

I have grown spiritually as I walked by faith with Christ, through my wilderness journey. I pray that my story will be instrumental in your spiritual growth and that it will help to teach you the essence of walking by faith. I have learned how to walk with faith and allow faith to take me by the hand (metaphorically). I have learned to walk with faith with the confidence of knowing that I will make it through the wilderness. In the words of an old gospel song "Lord hold my hands, while I run this race, because I don't want to run this race in vain".

It is my hope and prayer that you will be encouraged, as I am compelled by the Holy Spirit to share my testimony of my experiences and the challenges of my faith. It is my prayer that after you've traveled with me through my wilderness journey, you will see how determination and perseverance do pay off in the end, if you place your trust in the Lord.

I pray you will learn that keeping your eyes on Jesus in the midst of life's crises will strengthen your faith. When Peter saw Jesus walking on the water, Peter asked Jesus to allow him to come, Jesus said to him come and by faith Peter also walked on the water. As

3

long as Peter kept his eyes on Jesus, he was able to walk on water. But when Peter took his eyes off of Jesus and focused on the water that is when he began to sink

I pray that at the end of my wilderness journey, you will truly believe that when we say, "It ain't over until God says it's over," it is not just a cliché. I've learned that as long as you don't allow the adversary to distract you and prevent you from looking through your spiritual eyes and see Jesus, the Lord Jesus will not allow you to sink. Only through your spiritual eyes can you see the Lord Jesus hands reach out to you if you are drifting away. Only through your spiritual eyes can you see Jesus safety net beneath you to catch before the fall. Only through your spiritual ears can hear the voice of the Holy Spirit calling out to you with stretched out arms to pull you up before you sink too deep. I can relate to King David's cry in Psalm 40:-1-3 *¹I waited patiently for the Lord, He turned to me and heard my cry ²He lifted me out of an slimy pit, out of the mud and mire and set my feet on a rock and gave me a firm place to stand ³He has put a new song in my mouth, a hymn of praises unto our God. Many will see and fear the Lord, and put their trust in Him.*

There were many times that I briefly took my eyes off "The Mighty One" who would later answer my prayers. I felt myself sinking emotionally into a depression, and that's when we have to hold our heads up and look up to the hill from where our comes Psalm 121:1-2 *¹I will look up to the hills from where my help comes ²My help comes from the Lord, which made the heavens and the earth.*

When we say by faith God is an on-time God, we are expressing words that are drawn from our many experience when the Lord intervened on our behalf. It is the word of God that kept me through so many trials of life. That is reason why I am sharing with you the many scriptures that empowered me to keep fighting in spiritual warfare.

What we are saying is that the Lord steps in, just in the nick of time and at the right time although it wasn't according to my timing. Also, as you follow each of my wilderness steps, you will realize the importance of knowing how to spiritually discern when and if the Holy Spirit is speaking to your inner spirit. I pray that you will learn how to discern when you are being lead by the Holy Spirit on this Christian journey. There are many spirits but there is only one Holy Spirit communicating to believers and usually confirmed by a Christian Church leader/pastor, elder, bishop, Ect.

Knowing how to discern the inaudible voice of the Holy Spirit will help you avoid some of the trials of life. Sometimes we are the cause of our problems meaning we can bring some of our troubles upon ourselves. When we are being lead by the flesh and not led by the Holy Spirit, some trials of life will come and can take longer to end than necessary.

I learned my lessons the stressful and hard way because there were times when I allowed myself to be lead by the flesh. One way you and I can know how to discern when we are lead by the Holy Spirit we must study the word of God. 2Timothy 2:15 *the apostle Paul instructs us to "Study to show yourself approved, a workman needed not to be ashamed rightly dividing the word of truth."* If you study then you will know who He, the Holy Spirit is, and how He operates in the lives of believers. Paul also said *Faith comes by hearing and hearing the word of God Romans 10:17. Studying and hearing God's word will keep us and help us patiently wait, while God is working on our behalf.*

I pray you will learn that trusting in Christ is a necessity and that the patience of a believer in Christ is a virtue. The prophet Isaiah said, *"They that wait upon the Lord will renew their strength"* (40:31).

I pray that my story will help you through any wilderness life experience that you may encounter. It is my prayer that my story

5

will help you realize that each trial of life can be used as a measuring rod. It should be used as a measuring rod to see how far the Lord has brought you in your walk with Him. Your trials can be used as a scale to weigh how strong or deep within your faith may be. Your trials also can be used to objectively discern if you have grown spiritually enough to patiently wait on the Lord, no matter how long it takes, in times of adversity.

Biblical Symbols

In my book I have utilized as a symbol the Nation Israel's journey through their wilderness from Egypt to the Promised Land to help you visualize from my perspective my Christian journey. During my wilderness journey, I read Israel's story many times, which helped me get through some difficult times. It also helped me to appreciate that what we were going through as a local Church/congregation was nothing compared to their plight. Once again, I make no comparison of my journey to Israel's journey.

Here are the symbols I use:

- Moses symbolizes the leadership of a pastor/ under-shepherd.
- Israel symbolizes local churches and their fight against the adversary.
- Moses' father-in-law, Jethro, symbolizes the pastors who offered their help and support.
- The Jordan River symbolizes the many trials, troubles, and tribulations that we encountered.
- The wilderness symbolizes the roads that took us through two cities, Detroit and Highland Park.
- The mountain symbolizes the obstacles that were thrown in our path.
- The journey symbolizes the seven times we moved during the three years we were without a church building.
- Sheep or flock symbolizes the congregation.

Preparation for the Journey

Lord, what will you have me to do?

Acts 9:6

It was August 1982 when I strongly felt in my heart that just as the Lord called the apostle Paul on the Damascus road, He was calling me to preach His word. No, I did not hear an audible voice, but it was that inward burning that Jeremiah talked about, when he said "The word was like fire shut up in his bones" I had a deep, strong desire to teach and preach the Gospel of Jesus Christ. I was a deep burning that could only be quench by witnessing and sharing the word of God with others.

I answered, using the words of the prophet Isaiah: *"Lord, here I am, send me" (6:8). And in the words of the apostle Paul: "Lord, what will you have me to do"? (Acts 9:6).* I was eager and excited about being one of the Lord's vessels, or ministers. I was eager to preach in season and out of season. My call to preach was a midnight call while at work on the midnight shift. It was a quiet night shift at work with no one around just me and the Holy Spirit. After much meditation and prayer I finally surrendered to whatever the Lord's will was for my life.

Early that morning I first called my father and told him that I had surrendered to my call to preach. At that time my father was the assistant pastor of Galatian Missionary Baptist Church in Detroit, where I was serving as a deacon. I told my wife, Mary, and then my pastor at Galatian, Dr. H. W. Burroughs. Not one of them were surprised.

I believe that one's call to preach should be seen by the act of faith through his and her works. My faith had been on display for approximately six years by the way I served my Lord and Savior Jesus Christ, my pastor and my Church family.

Sometimes it is not clear what path the Lord has predestined for His sheep, but it was at this time when everything became very clear to me. There were signs that had been revealed to me as well as some hints concerning what I believe the Lord was showing me. I knew that I couldn't run away from the task that He had assigned to me. Finally, my thought was if God has predestined me to preach surely He will equip me for the work ahead.

August 1982 accepted my call to be a minister of the gospel but it was not until January of 1983 before I would preach my first sermon. Pastor Burroughs told me to inform him when I was ready to preach but nervousness and fear prevail for five months before I finally went to him. January 1983 after preaching my first sermon Pastor Burroughs officially licensed me a minister of the gospel of Jesus Christ.

I enrolled at Southern Baptist Theological Seminary of Biblical Studies because I wanted to be fully equipped to preach and teach the Gospel of Jesus Christ. I attend Bible College at 6 p.m. every Tuesday for three hours of class. While a student, I worked a full-time job—the midnight shift—at Henry Ford Hospital.

It was difficult going to school, working the midnight shift, and raising a family, but it paid off. In January 1987, I was ordained as a minister under the leadership of Pastor Burroughs. I wasn't in

a hurry to be ordained because my emphasis was directed toward understanding sound Biblical doctrine. Also I wanted to be an apologist, one who could defend the gospel of Jesus Christ. The adversary's strategy is seeking out believers that are Biblically illiterate Peter's words in his first letter is remain to believers of Satan's weapon of warfare. I Peter 5:7-8 *⁸Be alert/vigilant and be of sober mind. Your enemy the devil prowls around like a roaring lion looking for someone to devour ⁹Resist him, standing firm in the faith, because you know that the family of believers throughout the world is undergoing the same kind of sufferings.*

It was the latter part of 1986 when Pastor Burroughs' health began to fell him. I had honestly considered leaving Galatian because there were a few members who had already begun talking about me becoming the pastor of Galatian during Pastor Burroughs' illness.

I had some reservations whether I wanted to Pastor Galatian or any church. In the flesh I thought if I leave before Pastor Burroughs makes his transition, the congregation would have to select someone else. At the same time, I knew that I couldn't leave, knowing my pastor needed me there. Also the Lord had not shown or revealed to me another church to join. Sometimes it seems to be easier to run from responsibility than to take responsibility. I can accredit my staying the course to my father because he instilled so many values in me such as steadfastness.

Nowhere to run and nowhere to hide

On June 30, 1987, my beloved pastor, Dr. H. W Burroughs, made his transition. He was called home to be with the Lord, and that's when my true test of faith as a pastor began.

June 30th was the day that changed my life forever because the very responsibility that I wanted to run from became a reality. Approximately 3:30pm June 30th I received a phone call from one of the members of Galatian, informing that Pastor Burroughs had made his transition. I call it transition because we know that believers in Christ don't die but are transform in the moment of a twinkling of an eye I Corinthians 15:51-52

I was numb, deeply sadden, grieved stricken with so many thoughts running rampant in my mind. Pastor Burroughs had been a father figure to me as well as he was to other young men and women. He had certainly been my spiritual father and leader to so many but now he's gone. 27 years later I still think about him and how deeply he touched my life. If I needed anything I knew that I could always depend on him. All I had to do was call or go to him and ask.

Pastor Burroughs always called me Bill instead of Willie or reverend, like a father calling his biological son. I learned so much sitting under the feet of such a wise, caring, loving and generous pastor. There would not have been a Galatian nor would we have come this far without Pastor Burroughs vision. I wasn't sure if I could even begin to be the pastor that he was. I did know that I had to stand by the grace of our Lord Jesus and power of the Holy Spirit.

A few days later which was on that Friday after Pastor's death, the officers of Galatian called a meeting. They met to decide on who they wanted to be the interim Pastor of Galatian. They decided that I would lead Galatian until the congregation voted on a permanent Pastor.

Growing Up

Looking beyond my circumstances

When I reflect back on the day that I accepted the call into the ministry, I thought that all I had to do was just preach. Little did I know that the Lord would put me in the position as the pastor of one of His sheepfold, Galatian Missionary Baptist Church.

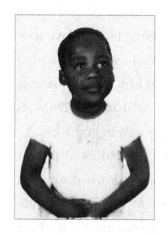

I grew up in a Christian home and I had a church home. My father, the Reverend John Willie Cleveland, was the pastor of a little storefront church, Guiding Light Missionary Baptist Church, with a handful of members. My mother, Inez Cleveland, my five brothers, five sisters, and I were all members.

We grew up in the Brewster-Douglass Projects on the east side of Detroit. The Brewster Projects were considered to be a village within a city. It was about a thirty-to-forty-minute walk to downtown Detroit. There were three things that all of the families had in common: our parents were hardworking people; we lived in attached brick units that looked alike and stood side by side, which we called the "row houses"; and we were poor. Yet as kids, we didn't know that we were poor. Many families were on welfare. These three things brought the families together as a village. We grew up with Diana Ross, Mary Wilson, and Florence Ballard. All three lived in the Brewster Projects.

In the winter, two of my brothers and I had to get up early on Sunday mornings and walk approximately three to four miles from the projects to my father's storefront church. Along the way we had to collect paper and wood to add with the coals stored at the Church to make a fire in the iron potbelly stove. I digress, it is my opinion that American Christians today are spoiled. Yes we have in most Church buildings central air, gas furnaces and hot water. But then we depend on wood and coal burning iron stove for heat and hand fans to keep us cool in the summer. Even as I look at my test of faith, I dare not compare it to our Christian brothers and sisters in Iraq, Syria, and other overseas country. Christians are literally dying for Christ name sake. As believers we should always try to keep our trials of life in spiritual perspective.

By the time my father, mother, my other siblings and the congregation arrived at church, the building would be warm. I can remember it being so cold in the building that the water in the bathroom bowl would freeze. We would open the bathroom door to allow heat inside until it was warm enough to thaw the water. How did we ever survive without a gas force air furnace and air conditioning in the summer?

My siblings and I went to church not by choice but by force, in other words we did have a choice. We sometimes laugh about it today. From my perspective as a kid, being in church from nine in the morning until nine in the evening every Sunday sometimes seemed to be punishment.

I didn't know then that growing up in church would someday help to mold me into the Christian man, husband, father, and pastor that I am today, although I am still striving for to reach perfection. When I think about it, my parents' faith in Christ demonstrated their strong, unwavering commitment to the Lord Jesus. Observing our parents walking by faith would later be instrumental in teaching my siblings and me the importance of trusting in the Lord.

By the examples they set, we learned how to walk by faith and not by sight. We learned that walking with faith means walking with Jesus Christ. My mother use to sing a song that I still sing from time to time "Walk with me Lord" She sang that song throughout her Christian life and it has become one of my favorite songs. She would sing walk with me Lord, walk with me. Walk with me Lord; walk with me while I'm on this tedious journey. I want Jesus to walk with me. Even now as I write these words, I can feel tears trying to permeate down my face.

My father was a hardworking Christian man, husband, father, and pastor. He instilled in me and my siblings the importance of a strong work ethic and the value of a dollar. We used to sell popsicles and ice cream on a stick. I use to ride a three-wheel ice cream bicycle or wagon throughout the entire Brewster Projects/village and beyond, selling popsicles and ice cream. I learned how to count money, which helped me to become very good in mathematics. There are still some old neighborhood friends I occasionally run into who call me "the ice cream man," although I was little boy at the time.

There was a neighbor who also sold ice cream who composed his own ice cream song which goes like this "It the ice cream man, it is the ice cream man, hay little kiddies playing in the sand go and tell your momma it's the ice cream man. One for a nickel and two for a dime, I would give you more but they ain't none of mind."

Watching my father taught me many valuable lessons, such as determination, staying the course, don't give up when facing adversities. I learned that an honest day's work will produce an honest day's pay. I learned from my father how to earn money the old-fashioned way—by working for a paycheck. My father as well as other fathers in the village epitomized the sign seen so often today by alleged homeless people "I'll work for food." The fathers in the projects most of them literally worded for food.

Through those lessons, I have adopted the saying: "No work, no pay, no pay, no eat, no eat, no live." Faith without works won't put food on the table. Faith without works won't put you in position to be blessed.

My father as well as the other fathers in the village epitomized the cliché of today: "I'll work for food. As tough as times were in the forties, fifties, and sixties, my father's faith and trust in the Lord gave him the strength to stay the course. He could have walked out on his family during those tough times, but he didn't. He stayed the course. I believe that it was his strong faith in Christ and commitment to his family that sustained him. It also taught me that no matter how strong the wind may blow, stay the course. No matter how challenging the task may appear to be, stay the course.

One of the greatest and most valuable lessons I learned from my father was to never give up trying to be better and to do better in life. My father taught me to look beyond my circumstances and see the salvation of the Lord. He taught me to try to envision the light at the end of the tunnel. He looked beyond the Brewster Projects. He saw himself and his family moving out of the projects. And in the summer of 1965, in the month of June, we moved out of the Brewster Projects. We moved into our own home on Dexter Street, on the west side of Detroit.

I look back and I'm glad my father and mother made us go to church because this is where our spiritual foundation began. But growing up in the Brewster Projects as the son of a pastor and preacher was not popular nor was it easy. Our neighborhood friends thought that we should act like angels because my father was a preacher. We were often called "the preacher's kids," and labeled as holier than thou. I must admit that I rebelled. I tried to show my friends that I wasn't an angel but that I was tough. My mission was to be the opposite of an angel. I would get into trouble in school and occasionally pick fights. Today they call it bulling and of course Jesus persona was not that of a bully. Bulling no matter what age is not Christ like. I would later learn that meekness is not weakness. As a Christian to be Christ like lovable does not mean that I am gullible.

One of the benefits my father had as a pastor was having eleven children which meant, he had his own home-grown choir. I was one of the lead singers in the Cleveland family choir. My brother David and sister Dian were also lead singers in the Cleveland choir. I also used to sing R&B during the doo-wop years which started in elementary school. I began to sing with several groups in junior and high school. My dream was to record a number one hit song and become famous. Of course, I wanted to make millions of dollars and live in a real mansion—not a mansion in the sky. I would learn later that the Lord God Jesus had other plans for my life. Also I must be honest and confess that I didn't have a real, true, sincere relationship with Christ. I knew about Him but I didn't really know Him, not until much later in life. Also my father didn't strongly object to me singing secular songs, not that it would have necessarily changed my course.

During the fifties and sixties, even the secular songs were more like love songs than songs are today. We had songs like "Stand By Me," "There goes my baby moving on down the line," "Get a job," and "I got a job. "Why do fools fall on in love," "Why don't you write me daring, send me a letter." Music was not ear killing and the words, or lyrics, to the songs were not so hardcore. But still secular songs that exalt the Lord Jesus.

It was a blessing to go the Arcadia skating rink on Woodward Avenue. We would walk several blocks to down Woodward to go to a movie, but we called it "going to the show." Popular places then were the Fox Theater, the Palms, and the Fine Art Theater. We were not allowed to go to the Gray Stone ballroom where many of friends went to dance/party. My father would on rare occasions take me to Briggs Stadium to watch the Detroit Tigers. We would walk to the stadium, which were approximately 7 or 8 miles away from the projects, but as a kid it seems that the walk was around 15or 20 miles.

From Sunday to Sunday, week after week, I had a front-row seat observing my father's faith being put to the test. I watched my father struggling and straining to keep the congregation together, struggling to keep the Church doors open. I knew how hard and difficult the task of pastoral ministry was, especially pastors of small local small congregations.

So many lessons I learned as a pastor and one of those lessons is this "It doesn't look so difficult when I was on the outside looking in. As I watch/observed pastors go through the fire. It didn't appear to be so hot. It was a different story after I became one of the Hebrew boys thrown into the fiery furnace (Metaphorically) As a matter of fact, when I was a little boy, my mother and siblings used to say to me, "Willie, you are going to be a preacher," and I would say, "NO WAY, JOSE." Why? Because I had seen the burning building, and I did not want to get burned. Being a preacher wasn't even a fleeting thought for me. I had learned that the expectations are too high for pastors to reach. Only a very few in the congregation truly appreciate the burden placed on a pastor's shoulders. Little did I know that growing up in the Brewster Projects and all the lessons my father taught us by example would become my driving force through my own wilderness journey as a pastor.

When I was called to preach the gospel of Jesus Christ, my first thought was, "Lord, I have brothers and sisters, why pick on me?" And I've wondered how did my mother know that the Lord had placed a calling on my life to preach the Gospel? I now believe it was because, according to her and others, I look so much like my earthly father—a preacher.

Sometimes it is not clear what path the Lord has predestined for His sheep but when everything became very clear, I then knew what the Lord wanted me to do. I knew that I couldn't run away from the task that had been assigned to me. There were signs that and hints revealed to me concerning what I believe the Lord was showing me. My thought was if God predestined me, surely He will equip me for work ahead.

Now Running for the Lord

Having the Jonah syndrome

Sometimes it seems to be easier to run from responsibility than to take responsibility.

After my decided to dissolve Guiding Light MBC, most of my family became members of Starlight Missionary Baptist Church. In 1980 we became members of Galatian Missionary Baptist Church. My father became the assistant pastor there, under the leadership of Dr. H. W. Burroughs. It was the latter part of 1986 when Pastor Burroughs' health began to fail.

In January 1987, I was ordained as an official minister of the gospel. At that time I was working as an assistant to my pastor at Galatian alongside my father. But I considered leaving Galatian during Pastor Burroughs' illness, because there were a few members who had begun talking about me becoming the pastor of Galatian.

After Pastor Burroughs made his transition, Galatian was left with two associate ministers, my father and me. The truth is my first thought was to run away to another local church because I wasn't sure if I could handle the responsibilities of being a pastor or if I wanted the hardship. I had the Jonah syndrome. I didn't know if I wanted to try to carry the tremendous load placed on a pastor's shoulders. But there was nowhere to run to and nowhere to hide from the call to pastoral duty. "Not my will, Lord, but your will be done."

I did not fully understand that if God put me to the test, God would carry me during and through the test. If it was God's for me to get thrown into the furnace (metaphorically) then God would keep me safe in the furnace. In other words, God would wrap me in a fireproof suit of protection.

I thought that my dad, Reverend John Willie Cleveland, would be the interim pastor until the congregation elected him as the permanent pastor. And, if they didn't choose my father, they would call in another pastor.

Well, my father was the kind of man who wanted very much to see me, his son, succeed and so he told the officers of the church, "I am an old racehorse with more years, miles, and energy behind me than I have in front of me. My son is a young racehorse and I want you to consider appointing him as interim pastor."

On June 30, 1987, due to the death of my beloved pastor, I became the unofficial interim pastor of Galatian Missionary Baptist Church.

In Moses' Shoes

Discernment

In the next few months, I spent a lot of time fasting and praying, asking the Lord to reveal to me that it was His will for me to become the full-time pastor of Galatian. I still wasn't 100 percent sure that I wanted to be pastor of Galatian or any of congregation. I can honestly say that I grew up spiritually in Galatian as a member. I believed that there were advantages as well as disadvantages if I became the pastor of Galatian.

The Advantages

The advantage was as pastor I knew what the congregation needed in order to grow spiritually, numerically, and financially. As pastor I evaluate the Church's progress by the spiritual growth of its membership, which can be seen and measured through seeing lives of sheep change for the better. One of the essentials in spiritual growth comes by way of studying the Word of God.

As members grow spiritually, most will become strong witnesses for Christ and bring or invite lost souls to the Church to be saved—their relatives, friends, neighbors, and coworkers.

The Word teaches us that as sheep/members bring in new sheep/members; this promotes numerical growth of a congregation.

As each member grows spiritually and then embraces God's plan of tithing to finance the Church, which promotes the church's financial growth.

When I became interim pastor of Galatian, the church was in the red financially. We were struggling to pay our bills. Contrary to what some folk want to believe, local churches cannot survive without the tithe and offering of the members. This is a problem in many small churches today. The lack of financial support from members makes it very difficult for a church to be the outreach community congregation that the Lord commissioned the church to be.

I believed that the Holy Spirit had allowed me to discern what changes were necessary to promote Galatian's spiritual, numerical, financial growth and progress. It was my observation that Galatian was lacking in all three. I knew that the changes I believed were necessary would not be popular. But the Lord didn't ordain pastors to be popular but strong leaders.

The Disadvantages

The disadvantage of a minister being called to pastor from within the congregation can be too familiar. Some of the members of a congregation had become too familiar with me as a minister. There are usually a few who found it to be difficult to make the transition, from accepting me as their pastor, the lay minister. And some who just were not willing to accept me the new pastor because I wasn't like the pastor Burroughs. I also believe that some are not willing to respect the position. When I was an associate minister, I was in the office of serving and following, but as pastor I would be called to the office of leadership. I was the same person but with a higher call and the responsibility to lead the sheep and not follow the sheep.

Pastors are chosen, or called, into office to lead the sheep/congregation and not be led by them. That was one of the many valuable lessons I learned during my journey in the wilderness.

Grass not greener

I also found out that leading looks easy when I was in passenger's seat. But after I was placed behind the wheel, the view was entirely different.

Someone told the story about the farmer who had a cow that kept jumping the fence because it thought the grass was greener on the other side, which meant that grazing would be greener on the other side. The farmer figured out that the cow didn't start jumping the fence until he painted the fence green. People look at pastors believing that they live the glamorous life, but once I became the pastor I realized that is was more work and less glamour. Also I reality would set in that someone painted the fence green between the lay minister and pastor. There is no glamour in preaching that the wages of sin is death but the gift of God is eternal life. Most want to hear about the gift but don't to hear about the sin. We live in a "God what have You done for me lately society" and not "God what will you have me to do?"

In November 1987, I was elected the permanent pastor with full-time responsibilities to lead the flock of Jesus Christ at Galatian. I was told that approximately 95 percent of the congregation, by their votes, said they wanted me—Rev. Willie E. Cleveland—to be their under-shepherd, their pastor.

As a lay member, I had observed Pastor Burroughs leading Galatian by example. I was in the car but sitting on passenger's side. It was an inside view. But now that I was the pastor, I soon realized that I didn't have a clear view of the emotional aspects of pastoring a congregation.

But the lessons came quickly.

My Test of Faith Begins

Honeymoon

My first great test of faith as a pastor came not in the church but in my family. I received a call from one of my siblings who informed me that my dad had a heart attack.

All of my youth, my father led me as my pastor. And now I had been blessed to have my dad as my assistant pastor for one year and eleven months. He helped guide me through my so-called "honeymoon period,"—the first two or three years of pastoring in a church. From a spiritual perspective, when a pastor is called or elected to a local church, it is looked upon as a marriage. Just as Jesus is married to the church universal, a pastor is "married" to the congregation, for better or worse.

Immediately after the "wedding," or the pastor's installation, the two parties have what is called a "honeymoon." It is a period of harmony, a time to establish a new relationship between the pastor and the congregation. I had to reestablish my position from the minister most knew as Rev Willie, one of pastor's pastor Burroughs associates minister. I had to become Pastor Willie Cleveland, the Joshua who was appointed to take Moses place. Now I cannot allow friendship or family relationship distract me from the changes that I knew were necessary to promote spiritual, numerical and financial growth.

After two or three years of harmony, the Adversary usually tries to cause division in the church. The Adversary attempts to break that harmonious relationship between the pastor and the congregation. My honeymoon period at Galatian lasted approximately two and a half years.

My father and my wife were my strongest supporters in the ministry. My father offered me the wisdom he had gained during his time as a pastor. Every Monday morning, my father and I would talk by telephone to discuss Sunday's worship service and the sermon that he, as assistant pastor, or I had preached. We often discussed the state of Galatian's spiritual, numerical, and financial growth or the lack thereof. We were a team. I grew as a pastor because I never knew too much when it came to talking to my father or other seasoned pastors I respected when I was a lay minister.

I never walk alone even after my father passed away because I also had my wife, Mary walking with me on the journey. Thanks to the Lord Jesus for giving me a strong, full-of-faith, Jesus Christ–believing wife. Mary was there from the beginning of my ministry, and she stuck close to me through that difficult week of my dad's death as we prepared for the home-going.

She supported and comforted me as I shed tears, grieving for my father. Who prays for the pastor/under-shepherd when the pastor is overwhelmed with grief? Usually there is a strong Christian wife interceding on his behalf. Mary was there for me and with me.

I've heard my father, mother, and other Christians say, "The Lord won't put any more on you than you can bear." As a child I really did not understand what that meant. During those long days leading to the home-going of my dad, my faith was put to a test beyond what I thought I could handle. But God carried my mother, my siblings,

Mary, and me through our dark days. The reality of those words became clear. I found out that those words were true.

I found out that God doesn't desert his children or allow us to walk alone. As the poem "Footprints in the Sand" says, when we are too weak to walk, God carries us. When we are not strong enough to stand on our own two feet, God becomes our leaning pole. When our hearts are broken up in grief, He is a heart fixer, and He does ease the pain. It took much prayer to get us through our devastation. But my faith and knowing that my father's salvation was assured gave me consolation.

One evening the Lord said to the Reverend John Willie Cleveland, "Well done, good and faithful servant. You have been faithful over a few things, and I'm going to make you ruler over many things."

The Lord called him home.

The Exodus

Now faith is [being sure of] what we hope for and
[certain] of what we do not see.
—Hebrews 11:1 NIV

After the home-going of my father, it was time for me to move on, and as difficult as it was, I knew I had a congregation to shepherd.

Many years ago, Pastor H. W. Burroughs preached a sermon with this message: "If it ain't one thing, it is another." I would soon know what that meant.

About a year after my father's home-going, some of the members of the church decided to leave and join other congregations. They did not agree with some pastoral decisions and changes I knew had to be made. Unfortunately they were not receptive to change but sometime changes in what local Churches are doing are necessary if there is no growth. Why keep doing the same thing if you keep getting the same negative results, especially if it isn't God's way?

I had been a member of Galatian ten years and had the benefit of discerning what didn't work. I knew that we could not continue doing business as usual. Even before the congregation elected me as pastor, I knew what changes I would have to make. Galatian was not a tithing church and I knew that had to change. We had been doing certain things to support the church for thirty-three years that didn't work: fashion shows, selling BBQ and fish dinners, car washes and so on. It didn't make sense to keep doing the same things and expect different results.

I viewed the members leaving the church as an exodus. I learned a very valuable lesson during this test of faith: Standing on the Word of God can and will cause an exodus in the church. The prophets of old put their lives on the line standing on God's words and principles. I believe that church leaders today must continue to stand on the foundation of the church, Jesus Christ, the Word. No matter who leaves the church, I learned very early in ministry that I can't or won't change God's Word to try to please people who really don't want to grow spiritually.

When I became pastor of Galatian in 1987, there were approximately 350 members, with 300 active members. During "the exodus" over a four-year span, the church decreased to approximately 150 members.

Emotionally, it really hit me hard when the members left. These were some of the same people who had cast their votes for me to become their pastor. These were the same people who told me after I was elected that they would work with me, they would become more active in church by serving wherever they were needed. Some stated they would stick with me through thick and thin. But when I started to make changes that they did not agree with, they began to move out.

I have learned that it is more painful for a pastor to watch sheep leave the fold than it is for the sheep to leave. Some if not most leave the fold without ever looking back. But a pastor after God's own heart will grieve for an extended period of time before being able to recover from the loss.

When members leave, it compels pastors to question whether the Lord is really walking with them. I believe that a truly caring pastor will always examine self first before looking at others. I questioned myself as to whether I was qualified to continue to lead. I felt that maybe it was something I said or did that was wrong. With a declining congregation, it was difficult not to question my own leadership ability. I even gave some consideration to resigning as pastor. Looking at a declining membership and after the death of my dad, my faith was shaky.

But I believed that with even a little faith and patience, the Lord would see me through this test of faith. I kept hearing an inaudible voice saying, "It is just a test." I discerned that the voice I heard was the Holy Spirit speaking to my inner spirit.

I finally came to believe that those who left did not leave Galatian for the right reasons. None of them said they were leaving because they weren't being fed spiritually. They left because they didn't want to follow the leader.

The Bible teaches us that our faith will be put to a test, sometimes to many tests. It is impossible for anyone to live an entire life without any trials or without their faith being put to a test. The important question that every believer should ask is, "Can I withstand the test?"

One More River to Cross

Don't you know that you yourselves are God's temple
and that God's Spirit lives in you?

1 Corinthians 3:16

I have read about the trials of Job many times, and although I dare not compare my test of faith to Job's there were times it seemed that I, just like Job, was experiencing one test after another. During my third year as pastor, even the church walls became a threat. One of the officers of the church brought to my attention the fact that the sanctuary walls were leaning which was dangerous.

A construction contractor examined the building and discovered that the walls were pulling apart from the roof, which could cause the roof to come tumbling down. The contractor installed three cable lines to hold the walls together temporarily.

Finally the board and I decided that our old church building was unsafe to continue using for worship services. I decided that we needed to raise enough funds to repair or rebuild our church.

We were blessed to have three buildings—the sanctuary, the fellowship hall, and the parsonage. Although all three buildings were old and in need of repairs, we decided that the fellowship hall was in good enough condition to have worship services until we could repair or rebuild our sanctuary. On December 31, 1990, we moved into the fellowship hall and had our first worship service there on New Year's Eve service in.

I learned after that move that some believers in Christ were building worshipers. Shortly after we moved into the fellowship hall, a few more members moved their membership to other churches. They could not handle the thought of worshiping in the fellowship hall nor would they invite their friends to come visit.

It was my hope that everyone understood the writings of the apostle Paul in 1Corinthians 3:16: *"Don't you know that you yourselves are God's temple and that God's Spirit lives in you?"* They did not understand that the building was not the church. They did not understand that the church is made up of the body of born-again believers. I was concerned about the members leaving. I don't know of any pastors who truly love the Lord who would not be concerned when sheep leave the fold.

The Adversary knows when your faith is wavering and when you are in pain. And he took a dagger and pushed it deeper into my wound. Just when I thought things couldn't get worse, guess what—things got worse to the point where I thought the church would not recover. Some neighborhood thieves broke into the fellowship hall, our worship building, and took whatever they could. What happened to the respect people use to have for the Lord's house?

I've learned that as long as we look through carnal eyes, we will never see God's spiritual truth. Walking by faith encompasses a trust, a confidence in the Lord that takes us beyond what our physical eyes can see.

Believers in Christ often testify about a blessing or healing that they are seeking from the Lord. Although they don't know how the

Lord is going to work that situation out, they will say, "The Lord will make a way somehow." Although we don't always know what method God is going to use, we believe that God is in the process of working out the problem.

Tougher Times Ahead

Trust in the Lord with all your heart and lean not on
your own understanding. In all your ways submit to
him, and he will make your paths straight

Proverbs 3:5–6

A few years after we moved into the fellowship hall, I came to the conclusion that the church had become stagnant. It seemed to me that the church had gotten too comfortable just being in the fellowship hall. We had done some renovating to make the space Church usable—new floor tile, drop-ceiling paneling, pastor's office, central air conditioning, and a cement sidewalk.

When we moved from the sanctuary to the fellowship hall, it was supposed to be just for a short time. It was supposed to be just long enough to raise enough money to remodel our old sanctuary, but the tithe, offering, and building funds decreased instead of increasing. It had been more than three years.

So in May 1994, I called for a general congregational meeting. A few days before the meeting, I sat down and wrote my letter of resignation. I believed then and now that if ever the time comes when the sheep won't respond to the pastor's leadership, it is time for the under-shepherd to move on.

Proverbs 3:5–6 teaches us to *"Trust in the Lord with all your heart and lean not on your own understanding. In all your ways submit to him, and he will make your paths straight".*

When you trust in the Lord, you will know that whatever the Lord has for you, no one can take it away. And so I believed that if it was the Lord's will for me to move on, He would speak through the congregation by way of their votes.

I have never been a quitter, but I thought if the congregation wanted new leadership, I will not stand in the way of the Lord's program. I had the letter read at the meeting, and then I took a poll (which again was a test of faith). I asked those who wanted new leadership to raise their hands. Not one person raised their hand.

The Adversary will beguile you into believing things will never get better if you allow him. But we must remember that Satan, the thief, comes only to steal, rob, and destroy. Faith knows that even when the things you pray about may be slow in coming or a no-show at the time, God is still in control. So don't throw in the towel.

Proverbs 16:3-5 *³Commit to the Lord whatever you do and He will establish you8r plans ⁴The Lord works out everything to its proper end. Even the wicked for a day of disaster ⁵The Lord detests all the proud of heart. Be sure of this: they will not go unpunished.*

I heard a minister state this "Some people don't plan to fell but some people fell to plan." I've learned the hard way that when our plans contradict God's plans, He will not bless in our plans. Earlier, while we were still worshiping in the main church sanctuary, I had presented to the congregation a five-year plan that would have raised $250,000. But because of the lack of faith and vision, the congregation voted the plan down. I truly believed that Lord had given me a plan but I also learned that it takes people who are willing to work the plan.

After the congregational meeting in 1994, I presented a new building fund plan, which was a five-month plan to raise money by selling barbecue, fried fish, chicken dinners, and car washes. We spent five months every weekend, from 9 a.m. to 5:30 p.m., selling dinners and washing cars, and all we did was break even. God's plan, or God's way, wasn't through selling ribs or chicken or fish dinners or car washes. I should have learned this from before, when the first members left.

You see, I also learned that a great test of faith comes by worshiping God through giving to His storehouse. We would have come out ahead if 30 members had given $10 each week, raising $300 a week. But there were some who didn't or wouldn't understand that giving is another test of faith. God had established the plan and so the Lord wouldn't bless that plan.

> *"Bring the whole tithe into the storehouse, that there may be food in my house. Test me in this," says the Lord Almighty, "and see if I will not throw open the floodgates of heaven and pour out so much blessing that there will not be room enough to store it.*
>
> —Malachi 3:10 NIV

I believe that one of the many tests of faith is when we are challenged with God's instructions to handle life's problems, trials, and tribulations God's way. We must show faith by being doers of the Word and not hearers only.

When the Adversary is trying to push us in the opposite direction, we must let Jesus lead us. I learned that selling dinners doesn't make up for a lack of tithe and offering. It teaches believers how to not trust the Lord for all of our needs. Also we had conformed to worldly system instead of being transformed by the renewing of our minds.

In Romans 12:1-2, the apostle Paul says *¹Therefore, I urge you, brothers and sisters, in view of God's mercy, to offer your bodies as a living sacrifice, holy and pleasing to God – this your true and proper worship ²Do not conform to the pattern of this world, but be transformed by renewing of your mind. Then you will be able to test and approve what God's will is – His good, pleasing and perfect will.*

On Fire

At 1:30 a.m. on Saturday, September 10, 1994, my phone rang. One of my trustees informed me that someone had set the fellowship hall—the place where we were worshiping—on fire. I immediately got out of bed, put on my clothes, and drove to the church on the west side

of Detroit. When I turned the final corner, I saw the fire trucks, the smoke and the flames coming from the burned-out fellowship hall.

I was not surprised. But it broke my heart. I call those who allow themselves to be used against the church "Satan's agents." I had warned the Galatian members "Do not be surprised when things like this happen."

Before the fire, enemies of the church had been attacking the physical church building. They stole aluminum siding off the sanctuary, broke into the unoccupied parsonage, and several times broke into the fellowship hall. Thieves took a computer, adding machine, office supplies, and parts of our sound system— whatever they thought they could sell. If it wasn't locked up or nailed down, they took it. We had been proactive in fighting to get drug activity out of our community, and I believe the fire was the result of that effort.

First Peter 5:8–9 says, *"Be sober, be vigilant; because your adversary the devil walks about like a roaring lion, seeking whom he may devour. Resist him, steadfast in the faith, knowing that the same sufferings are experienced by your [brothers] in the world"* (NKJV).

Sometimes when we are under the attack of the Adversary, both physically and spiritually, some of us think that we are the only ones under attack. But during that same period, several churches in the South were set on fire. Now I don't believe that the perpetrator who set our building on fire was racially motivated, but nevertheless, we were under attack.

Growing up in the Brewster Projects helped me to become tough both mentally and physically. Growing up in the church through the preaching and teaching of the Word of God in Christ gave me strength spiritually. As I looked at our church, still smoldering, I decided there was no way I would allow the devil to kill, rob, and destroy the hard work that Dr. H. W. Burroughs and my father and I had invested in Galatian.

Faith said, "Too much time has been sacrificed." Faith said, "Too many lives and families will be negatively affected if I allow the enemy to win." Faith said, "Don't give in."

But Fear said, "You can't do it."

And Faith said, "The Lord will bring you through it."

The Adversary can destroy the physical building, but he can't destroy my faith. Nor would I allow him through this devastation to destroy my hope, because in the words of Isaiah, *The Lord God is my hope* Isaiah 41:10. If ever I had to trust in the Lord with all my heart and lean not to my own understanding, now was the time. Although I didn't understand why the Lord allowed the fire to happen, I had to trust in the Lord. (Note: I didn't say the Lord *caused* the fire, but *allowed* the fire.)

As I stood there looking at the devastation from the fire, one of my faith trustees, Lew Dent approached me and, as we embraced, tears ran down my face. After the fire had been put out, I took a heartbreaking walk through the shell of what had been a beautiful church building. All of the love, sweat, tears, and hard work we surrendered to the Lord had been destroyed. My pastoral robes, choir robes, the pews, organ, drums, and office furniture were destroyed. The kitchen where we served many hot meals to the seniors in the community was unrecognizable. While standing in what once was our sanctuary, I looked up and I could see the sky through the enormous hole caused by the fire.

It reminded me of Psalm 121:1: *"I will lift up my eyes to the hills—from where my help comes?" (NIV).*

Sometimes we can allow obstacles to cloud our view and distort our vision from seeing the Lord, who is our present help in times of trouble.

In the flesh I cried out, "How could anyone disrespect the Lord's house, setting it ablaze!"

When the church is striving and pressing onward to do what is right, that is what compels the Adversary to try to steal, rob, kill, and destroy. We weren't a light hidden under a basket. We tried to make our neighborhood better. We tried to win souls for Jesus Christ. We had a community hot meals program five days a week called "Four Corners." We offered sewing classes for seniors. We offered GED classes, adult education programs, and a youth program.

I had been teaching the congregation that we the church universal and local are in a spiritual war against Satan. Not too long before the fire we had called the police to report drug activity in the area. The Adversary didn't want our little local church chasing away customers or making too much noise.

Sometimes I sing the song, "I've learned how to suffer for if I suffer I will gain eternal life." It is one thing to sing about suffering, to sing about faith. But it is harder to live by faith in your suffering. I understand now that my faith in Christ was carrying me through my suffering.

First Stop

Come, we can worship together

There is an old saying: "You never miss your water until your well runs dry."

Just the thought that our church building had burned down sent chills through my body. I can still remember the hurt, pain, and anger I felt as I looked that night at what was just a shell of our fellowship hall. I thought, "We can't go back into the sanctuary for worship service on Sunday." I likened going back into the old sanctuary to Israel going back to Egypt.

God brought Israel out of Egypt, but some of them wanted to go back into bondage. (Now, I must inject in here that in no way was I comparing our plight to Israel's suffering.) Galatian's old sanctuary was unsafe and too dangerous for anyone to be inside. I believed that maybe the Lord allowed the fire to get us out of our comfort zone. (Note again: I didn't say the Lord *caused* the fire, but *allowed* the fire.)

Yet I didn't want the congregation to miss a Sunday of worship. So when I arrived back home about 3:30 that morning, I called my good friend, Pastor Alex Whiteside, the pastor of a small local church, Antietam Missionary Baptist Church. Alex and I went to seminary together and had become very good friends. Our two local congregations had been having fellowship twice a year. We would visit each other's church buildings and worshiped together.

I told him about the fire and how everything was destroyed. I told him that we didn't have a place to worship.

Alex didn't waste any words. He said, "Come, we can worship together, both congregations, simultaneously sharing. You and I can share the pulpit. My church building is your church building. My pulpit is your pulpit because it belongs to the Lord."

Through his actions, my friend and brother epitomized what true friendship means. Some professed Christians talk about Christ, but a true born-again believer walks Christ. When things got thick, Alex didn't thin out on me.

That Saturday morning the call went out to the Galatian's congregation to explain what the Adversary had done to our fellowship hall. They also were informed that Galatian would be worshiping with Antietam Missionary Baptist Church on 24th Street, just a few blocks away from our home on Roosevelt Street.

The next day, both churches crowded into that small Antietam sanctuary and worshiped together for three consecutive Sundays. We had a shouting, worshiping good time, uplifting the name of Jesus.

Many Trials

If it ain't one thing, it is another

As I think back to my time of trial, I am once again reminded of a sermon that Dr. Burroughs preached: "If it ain't one thing, it is another." His sermon was about one of the many trials of Job. His sermon was about how one bad thing after another happened to Job and how Job's faith was put to a test.

Although my test of faith was never as severe as Job's, I can relate to Job's experiences. In 1976, our youngest daughter passed away at the age of thirteen. Our oldest son passed away in 2003 at the age of forty-four. Six months later, our grandson had been in a motorcycle accident and he too passed away at the age of twenty. And my father-in-law, who was also a member of Galatian, made his transition.

While my faith as well as the faith of my wife, Mary, kept being put to the test, in all of this, neither she nor I ever blamed God. As a matter of fact, even in the midst of our heartaches and pain, we continually worshiped and praised the Lord. To a non–believer, faith might seem strange, because when a Christian's faith is put to a test, we don't praise the Lord less, we praise Him more, we thank Him for lifting us up and keeping us to the end of each test. There are too many believer's in Christ are being misled through the teaching that Christians are not supposed to suffer.

The late Dr. .H.W. Burroughs often declared "If you have been through anything meaning trials, just keep on living' Also many think since we are Christians that we are exempted for the troubles, trials and tribulations. It was Jesus who said to His disciples "Although you are of the world, you are in the world" I surmised from Jesus's words to His disciples are meant for us believers today. He is saying that we can't escape all of the problems that come with living in this imperfect society.

Many professed believers in Christ Jesus pray, asking God to give them patience. They pray asking the Lord to increase their faith, but they are not willing nor do they want to go through the experiences or trials that produce patience and faith.

At my other job Henry Ford Hospital health Systems I am on the safety committee Whenever I am assigned to give an employee the "flag," which designates that employee to execute the Code Red/ fire drill procedure. I walk him or her through the drill. The reason I walk them through the drill is because I don't want them to fail the test.

Whenever the Lord allows us, His children, to be put to a test, He always walks us through the drill because the Lord doesn't want us to fail the test.

I can say that as difficult as it was going through so many tests of faith, I always had the reassurance of knowing that Jesus He was walking me through the tests. In Matthew 28:20, Jesus promises us: *Lo, I am with you always, even unto the end of the world.*

Second Stop

Consider it pure joy ... whenever you face
trials of many kinds

James 1:2:

Our next stop on our journey through the wilderness was a humbling experience for me. We rented the basement of Goodwill Community Christian Church on East Seven Mile in Detroit. We were now worshiping in a basement and my office was the men's restroom.

Faith continued to say, "The glass is half full, not half empty."

If Jesus can humble Himself and become a little lower than the angels and take on flesh, if Jesus can be born and placed in a cattle trough, which is the epitome of humility, surely the men's restroom is just a small act of humility.

And I believed that the Holy Spirit would always remind me of James 1:2: *"Consider it pure joy ... whenever you face trials of many kinds" (NIV).*

And so I would say, "Thank you, Lord, for providing Galatian a building to worship in."

Third Stop

Now faith is substance of things hoped for and the evidence of things not seen."

Hebrews 11:1

We moved again in April 1995—back to 24th Street. The Lord had blessed Antietam Missionary Baptist Church with another building on West McNichols Street. I believe that their building was a confirmation of Jesus' words to the two stewards, or servants, who wisely used the talents that their Master had entrusted to them: *You have been faithful over a few things, I will make you ruler[s] over many things* (Matthew 25:21, 23 NKJV).

Pastor Whiteside (I call him my Jethro because **as with Moses, his father-in-law** Jethro, comfort, counseled and help Moses through trying times.) Pastor Whiteside and his congregation opened up their hearts and doors to us once again. They had shared with us what they had, and the Lord rewarded them for their good stewardship with another building—donated, mortgage free. We moved into their old building.

The trials of life teach us that by faith, you can't beat God's giving, no matter how hard you try.

We were back on 24th Street, and I compelled to a ground-breaking ceremony on our property on Roosevelt Street to show that we were walking by faith according Hebrews 11:1: *Now faith is substance of things hoped for and the evidence of things not seen.*

Although there were only vacant lots on our property (the buildings had been razed), an official ground-breaking was saying that we or I could see the construction of a new building, spiritually speaking. Little did I know how long it would be before anything would happen. My faith allowed me to believe the Lord in what we hoped for and. Through my spiritual eyes I could see a new building although it had not come to pass. I dared not to look through my carnal eyes because I might have given up. But my faith and trust in the Lord became my driving force. As believers we press onward because we truly believe that there is a light at the end of the tunnel.

During my battles with doubts I believe that it was the silent whisper of the Holy Spirit (metaphorically) saying move forward and done look back. After I rededicated my back to Christ I dare not look back at worldly life I lived for the fear of getting pulled back.

Fourth Stop

*How good and how pleasant it is for [brothers] to
dwell together in unity!*

Psalm 133:1

Have you ever experienced during your Christian walk what seems as
if the Adversary just keeps knocking you down? Every time you get
up, before the count of ten, he knocks you right back onto the canvas.

That's how I felt. Before we could really get settled in the
building on 24th Street, the new owners locked us out. I never
completely understood the reasons. Before we moved in, I knew that
Pastor Whiteside was in the process of selling the building, with my
blessing. We were led to believe by the new owners that we could
lease the building from them. We were having our Bible studies
every Wednesday, and it was on a Wednesday when I discovered that
the new owner had changed the locks on the doors.

Once again, I called my friend and brother, Alex Whiteside, and
informed him of what had transpired. He said, "Move in with us."

Just like Jed Clampett of *The Beverly Hillbillies*, we loaded up our
stuff and moved away from 24th Street. Galatian's next destination
was to West McNichols Street with my friend Alex Whiteside and
his congregation, Antietam Missionary Baptist Church.

There were some who thought it would not work to bring
together two pastors, sharing the same pulpit. They could not believe

that two local congregations could worship together every Sunday for an extended period of time. They told Pastor Whiteside that he was making a big mistake.

But I am proud to say that Antietam and Galatian proved them wrong. It was understood that Pastor Whiteside was pastor of Antietam and I was the pastor of Galatian. If there were any issues, both congregations were instructed to take them to their respective pastor or deacons. There was unity and strength between Alex and me as well as with both congregations.

We praised, worshiped, and fellowshipped together from June 1995 to August 1996. Pastor Whiteside and I shared the pulpit. He would preach one Sunday, and I would preach the next Sunday. Our ministers, deacons, choirs, ushers, nurses, and youth ministry all served together.

We were living Psalm 133:1 *How good and how pleasant it is for [brothers] to dwell together in unity!*

Then in April 1996, Pastor Whiteside had a heart attack, and he too made his transition from this wicked society that we live in to that glorious place in heaven. Although I knew where he was, my friend's transition broke my heart.

Shortly after the home-going service for Pastor Whiteside, Antietam elected his son Rev. Reginald Caldwell as their pastor. Pastor Caldwell reassured me that we could stay there as long as we needed to stay. He told me that we could take as much time as we needed. He never made Galatian or me feel like we were not wanted there. They never made us feel as if they wanted us to hurry and move out of their building.

Pastor Caldwell and I continued to share the pulpit, preaching every other Sunday. Our two local congregations grew closer as brothers and sisters in Christ Jesus. The hymn "There is not a friend like the lowly Jesus, but there were two in my life who manifested Christ-like characters."

Both Pastor Alex Whiteside (my Jethro) and Pastor Reginald Caldwell (my brother) proved to be true friends. I don't think that I will ever find adequate words to express how grateful I was for the warm hospitality they both had shown me and my church family.

Finally, I decided that Galatian had become too comfortable worshiping with Antietam. I kept reminding Galatian that we didn't come to stay; we just came to spend "the night" at Jethro's place (Pastor Whiteside's church). But some of Galatian's sheep had unpacked and were ready to move in permanently. Some of Antietam's members were trying to convince me and the members of Galatian to stay. We were losing our way. It was time for us to move on. Imagine what would have happened if Abraham had stopped and settled in a place that God had not ordain. I truly believed that it was the Lord's will for Galatian to go back on Roosevelt Street. Although we had started building a new building, I knew that we had to move.

Proverbs 3:5–6 tells us to *Trust in the Lord with all your heart and lean not on your own understanding. In all your ways submit to him, and he will [direct] your path (NIV).*

Fifth Stop

One of the greatest tests of faith is to be in a situation where you can't see any way out or an answer to the problem. It had been approximately two years since Galatian had been out in the wilderness, and we still were not able to secure a mortgage loan to build a new church. It seemed as if there was just one obstacle after another, one closed door after another, one rejection after another.

My favorite Scriptures became *The Lord is my light and my salvation* (Psalm 27:1), *Wait on the Lord [and] be of good courage* Psalm 27:14, and *Trust in the Lord* (Proverbs 3:5).

I had contacted a realtor and asked him to show me some church buildings that were for sale. If you are not sure that the Holy Spirit is leading you, you will find yourself traveling in a different direction than the Lord has planned and mapped out for you.

Fear kept speaking to me. It said, "Rent a place or buy another building."

Faith said, "If you believe that the Lord is leading and guiding you, stay the course." Without faith it is impossible to please God, for he that comes to God must believe that He rewards those who seek Him.

One of my deacons, Lew Dent (I call him my Peter), quoted a proverb that stuck with me through my wilderness journey and even today: "If you know where you are going and you don't change direction, you will get there."

On Roosevelt Street, we had three paid-for lots, a history of hard work, and a reputation for being a light on that corner. There was no other place to go but to go back home to Roosevelt Street.

Although Galatian and Antietam worshiped together in unity, I came to the conclusion that we had gotten too comfortable. I prayed about it and felt strongly that the Holy Spirit was allowing me to see that it was time to move again.

I had been looking for another building to rent and I found a little storefront about a mile farther north on McNichol. Now I am concern about how the congregation would react to my news that we were moving again—not back to our home on Roosevelt Street but just a few blocks away. This would be our fifth move in two years on our way "home." I am sure some it probably didn't make sense to move down the street when we could stay where we were until we rebuild. I have read the Bible from Genesis to Revelation and I have never read where the Lord instructed the sheep/congregation to lead the under-shepherd/pastor. I had to lead Galatian whenever I felt compelled by the Holy Spirit. Also sometimes pastors have to exercise common sense and I saw the move as one more step closer to home.

The constant theme that I tried to convey to Galatian with each move was that we are on our way home. I felt that if the congregation truly believed that we were on our way back home, it would make moving again a little easier to accept, even if getting back home takes longer than expected.

My greatest concern, second to rebuilding, was keeping the congregation together. I did not want to lose anyone. I was afraid that some would leave if I moved them again. But if I truly believed that the Holy Spirit was leading me, then Psalm 27:1 must apply: *Whom shall I fear?*

And so we moved into a small storefront building on McNichol that held about ninety people, which was just a little small for us. I explained to the congregation that we were only going to be there for a short period of time.

Unfortunately, the time was even shorter than I thought it would be.

Sixth Stop

Here we go again

The building on McNichol had a room for worship, It had two one-toilet-and-sink restrooms and we were allowed to use only one. It had a small office, at least I didn't have use the restroom for an office because it had a small office that I was allowed to use. There were only two doors/entrance and exits, a front door, a back door. The back door had an iron security gate. The owner kept the back door security gate locked during the times we were using the building. I was not allowed to have a key, which caused me very great concerned. I had to protect the sheep/Galatian

If there had been an emergency, such as a fire, or if we needed to get out of the back door for any reason, we would be trapped inside the building. It was also against the fire code to lock a security gate while occupied. I tried several times to explain that to the owner, but he would not agree to give us a key.

I tried for approximately two months to convince the owner to issue me a key to both doors and allow us access to both restrooms. He refused. So for the sixth time, we had to move.

"Here we go again" is what the Adversary kept whispering in my ear. "Why haven't your blessings come through?"

I am sure you've heard the old saying, "An idle mind is the devil's workshop." Well, my mind was never idle, but it didn't stop the negative thoughts from creeping in.

We again loaded up our stuff and, looking much like *The Beverly Hillbillies*, moved away from the storefront on McNichol Street to a room in Highland Park, Michigan on West Grand Street. I had met a pastor, Elder Ernest Bruton who had very large Church building. He had a small room that was large enough for Galatian to have worship services and Bible study. We rented the room where we held our Sunday morning worship and Bible study.

Doubts

Faith is seeing with your spiritual eyes

Our journey through the wilderness had been going on for two years and two months. We kept praying and believing and trusting that the Lord to intervene on our behalf. By faith we continued to believe that we would return home. But on Roosevelt Street, where our sanctuary, parsonage, and fellowship hall used to stand, all three buildings were gone. There was nothing there but the vacant lots with a hole in the ground, a parking lot, and a fence.

My constant theme during our journey was: *The Lord is my light and my salvation; whom shall I fear?* (Psalm 27:1) and *Trust in the Lord with all your heart* (Proverbs 3:5 NIV).

I knew that I had been engaging in an ongoing battle with the Adversary. I kept thinking that the congregation was going to scatter, that they were losing their confidence in my leadership. We had moved from one place to another, and I was very concerned that the congregation had become weary. I never uttered the words to Galatian but because I had become a little weary. I could not allow them to see fear or doubt on my face. Many weeks, I had to fake it on Sunday morning or at Wednesday Bible study. I could not allow them to think that I had lost hope.

I remember telling one of the members that I was starting to have doubts whether we were ever going be in a position to rebuild. His reply was, "Pastor, if you have some doubts, how are we supposed to think or feel?"

That statement reminded me that if I lost my trust, faith, hope, and confidence in the Lord, the congregation would lose their trust too. I had to be strong no matter what.

> *Submit yourselves therefore to God. Resist the devil, and he will flee from you.*
>
> —James 4:7

And so I would sing or proclaim, *The Lord is my light and my salvation; whom shall I fear? The Lord is the strength of my life; of whom shall I be afraid?* (Psalm 27:1).

I wasn't standing alone. There is an old saying, "Behind every successful man is a good woman." But I want to correct that saying: "Standing *beside* this pastor was and is a Christian, God-fearing, fervent-praying, and full-of-faith, Holy Ghost–filled strong woman, wife, mother, and sister in Christ. My wife, evangelist Mary Cleveland, was the one constant voice gently speaking words of encouragement. She unceasingly would say, "Honey, everything is going to be all right."

I had enough pressure on me as it was, and can you imagine if she had responded like Job's wife did? "Why don't you just give up the vision, why don't we let the sheep scatter and just join another church?"

But Mary's faith and loyalty to me, her church family, and her Lord never allowed her to utter negative words. What I really didn't consider or even gave thought to was this anything that affected me also affected Mary.

During those three years of wandering in the wilderness, I went without a salary from the church because we had to rebuild the Lord's house. We had been in the process of buying a condo, but after the fire, we put our plan on hold.

We both agreed that we would not allow anything to get in the way of rebuilding the Lord's house.

The sacrifices that Mary and I made were made in the best interests of Galatian, and we never complained. She never complained about the two of us having to wait to buy and move into a new home. Because of that and so much more, she is deserving of special honor. Sometimes a pastor's wife does not get recognition for being a hard worker in the church. I can truthfully say that with the spiritual strength of Mary and the Holy Spirit holding me up, I was able to press onward.

Through our travel in the wilderness, there were many journeys of disappointment. One bank after another said no. One lender after another said no. Doors were closed in my face, leaving me with no hope of securing a loan to rebuild.

I'd hear a strange voice in the wilderness saying, "I told you so." It was the same voice that tempted Jesus in the wilderness after Jesus had fasted forty days and forty nights.

But through it all Mary was always there with words of encouragement. She kept saying, "Hold on to your faith" She would remind me of the sermons I had preached about faith. I had preached about seeing the light at the end of the tunnel. But there were times in the flesh when I couldn't see any light.

It is easier to preach and teach faith than it is to live faith. It is easy to tell someone else to hang in there. It was not easy when I found myself having to hold on.

There were many Sundays that I dreaded going to church because I didn't have any good news or any idea when or if we were going to rebuild. Many days and nights I became depressed and eventually was at an all-time low emotionally. But Mary would say, "Honey, it is going to be all right. The Lord will make a way somehow."

"Keep holding on"

I remembered when I was a little boy in gym class; we had to climb a rope from the floor to the ceiling. It was always easy to cheer my classmates when they were climbing the rope. But when it was my time to climb the rope, I discovered that it was hard. Every time I grabbed for a new spot on the rope as I climbed, it became harder and harder. But I heard my classmates shouting "Keep going! You are almost to the top of the rope!" And I would keep climbing until I reached the top. Sometimes on this Christian journey the trials of life can appear to be like a tall mountain. I've learned that if I keep climbing, don't let go and don't stop I will reach the top of the mountain

While traveling through the wilderness, not knowing if we were ever going to secure a mortgage loan to rebuild, I thought about that rope. I compared securing a loan to climbing that rope in junior high school and not knowing if I could or would reach the top. It reminded me of how easy it is to say to others, "Hold on to your faith."

Yet it is our faith that becomes our cheerleader. Our faith tells us to "keep climbing; you are almost at the top." And so I kept pressing forward and believing that one day we would secure a loan to rebuild our church.

Faith is seeing with your spiritual eyes and knowing that things are going to work out somehow. Faith believes that God has control and that God is always in control. As believers, we must understand that God will make a way somehow. Faith says, "God *is* the *somehow.*" We just don't know when or how.

Many times I was drained emotionally and weak physically, but Mary and I leaned on each other as we leaned on the Lord. The Holy Spirit would bring back to my memory that the Lord had already made a way, just as I had preached in many sermons.

That is what faith is, seeing God working on our behalf. Faith is seeing spiritually the finished product before deciding to tough it out physically. Hebrews 11:1 teaches us: *Now faith is substance of things hoped for, the evidence of things not seen.*

After our buildings on Roosevelt were demolished, there was no longer anything physical to touch with my hands or physical to see with my physical eyes. There was nothing but the three lots with a hole in the ground, a parking lot, and a fence.

But through my spiritual eyes, my faith allowed me to see a building—our new church building on that land—God's finished product.

Wait on the Lord

Beware of how much trust, faith, and confidence
you place in man.

One of the many lessons I learned during my wilderness journey was
to wait on the Lord and to wait patiently. I learned that lesson the
hard way, by not waiting.

During the first year after the fire that destroyed our fellowship
hall, I was introduced to *"get your money"* broker who guaranteed
that they could get us financing for a mortgage loan. The company
appeared to be legitimate. The office was located in a beautiful
building. But ... and there's always a "but" the company required a
$10,000 broker's fee on deposit in order to start the loan process. We
had some insurance money from the fire, but not enough to complete
the project, so I used that money for the deposit. The company gave
me what is called a "good faith letter of intent."

Beware of how much trust, faith, and confidence you place
in man.

Then I talked to a builder about starting the building project
while we were waiting to close on the loan for the mortgage. I was
concerned that the congregation had become restless. We decided
to start building the church foundation, the parking lot, and a fence
while waiting to close on the loan. I was thinking that by the time

the contractor finished phase one, we would have closed on the loan and could start phase two, the sanctuary.

Well, we lost the $10,000. And we didn't have any money left to finish the building project.

The mortgage broker, who had been highly recommended to me, was a fraud. I learned there were other victims of this same mortgage brokerage company. I testified against the company before the Attorney General, hoping we would get our money back. Unfortunately, we didn't recover any of the funds we lost. Sometimes life's lessons can be costly—financially, physically, and emotionally.

I have always been a very proud man, and I didn't want anyone to know that I was a victim of fraud. But I had to eventually tell the congregation that I had given away $10,000. I feared that even though the congregation had stuck with me, this loss might be too much for them to accept. But, thank the Lord, we got past that difficult time and moved on.

The Unthinkable

I had taken my eyes off of God

I never told anyone, not even Mary, but on my journey through the wilderness, I considered committing suicide.

I felt as if all hade had broken loose and I had nowhere to turn. Emotionally, I was so depressed; I was at my lowest ever.

That's how the devil works. He spiritually attacks believers in Christ. He spiritual attacks the mind. But even at my lowest, I recognized that I was engaged in spiritual warfare. I knew that committing suicide was against God's will. The Holy Spirit reminded me that Jesus came to earth and took upon Himself flesh. Jesus bled, died, and rose from the grave so that you and I might have life.

Jesus didn't give His life so that those of us who claim to belong to Him can take our own lives, commit suicide. How can God get any glory out of a believer life in Christ if he or she taking his or her own life? He can't.

The apostle Paul instructed believers to *present your bodies [as] a living sacrifice* (Romans 12:1).

I had quoted Proverbs 3:5–6 many times, yet at that very moment of suicidal thoughts, I was leaning to my own plan and understanding, not God's. I had stopped trusting in the Lord. I had taken my eyes off of Him. When we devise our own plan—and suicide certainly was my plan— I refer to that as taking our eyes off the Lord and leaning to our own understanding. It is also a sad reality that sometimes pastors can be too focusing on feeding and helping the flock. We put so much of ourselves into what the flock need that we don't recognize when we are in need of help. Every born again believer in Christ should have at least one pray partner that we trust and can call upon during the critical times of the trials of life. It is also unfortunate that some pastors can feel like alone soldier with nowhere or no one to turn to during our spiritual battles.'

The Apostle Paul acknowledged that he wasn't superman or super apostle and that he had become weak. The lesson we all can draw from his experiences is this after realizing how weak he was, he called upon the name of the Lord for help II Corinthians 12:7-9 He declares *⁷Because of these surpassingly great revelations, therefore, in order to keep me from becoming conceited, I was given a thorn in the flesh. A messenger of Satan, to torment me ⁸Three times I pleaded with Lord to take it away (The thorn in the flesh) from me ⁹But He said to me, "My grace is sufficient for you, for My power is made perfect in weakness, therefore I will boast all the more gladly about my weakness, so that Christ's power may rest on me.*

I had acquired a large personal life insurance policy and was thinking that if I commit suicide, the church could cash in the policy. Then there would be enough money to finish the building project. It wasn't well thought out because it was my plan and not God's plan for my life. God's plan was for me to live and lead Galatian back home.

I believe that suicide is actually a very selfish act. It is also my belief that people who commit suicide don't consider how many hearts are broken by their suicide. Some family members and close friends never recover from such a final act. I had to consider how devastating that would be to Mary, to our children, and to our

Galatian family. After giving it more scriptural and spiritual thoughts, I concerned this "How can I faced my Lord Jesus who gave His life after I selfishly take my life? This is how believers must fight the Satan, by using the word to talk ourselves out committing sin of any kind, especially suicide.

I have often asked the question, "Who is praying for the under-shepherd/pastor while the under-shepherd is praying for the sheep?" It is important for pastors to have someone in whom we trust to receive Godly counsel, considering the load we carry. Pastor and lay believers in Christ must be careful that we don't allow pride to be the cause of our demise.

I can't count how many times I woke up in the middle of the night in a panic because I had dreamed about how all of the insurance money from the fire was gone due to fraud. I didn't want to think about my decision to prematurely start phase one of the building project. We were out of funds and we couldn't get a loan to complete the project. "But God"

Over on Roosevelt Street, all we had was a hole in the ground that filled with water when it rained, a parking lot, and a fence around the property. There is an old saying: "The Lord takes care of babies and fools." Well, I wasn't a baby but by my own admission, I was foolish to start a building project before all the funds were secured.

Just the thought of not being able to finish the building project was embarrassing and that was my pride kicking in. What would the pastors and preachers in the city say about my leadership? And yes, there were some who were part of the exodus who would drive by the location laughing at this dumb pastor.

A word of cause to all believers in the Lord "Be very careful to whom you are hearing to speak to you. It is my belief that in today's time there are too many believers who are proclaiming that Lord spoke to them to the Lord told them. It couldn't have been the Holy Spirit speaking to me compelling me to start building prematurely. It was my lack of patience to wait on the Lord and fear of losing the flock that moved me. Many Christians have gotten themselves into trouble because that thought the Holy Spirit was speaking to them. We must learn how to try the Spirit by the Spirit to see if it is of God.

Galatian 3:3 *Are you so foolish? After beginning by means of the Spirit, are you now trying to finish by means of the flesh?*

I John 4:1 *Dear friends, do not believe every spirit, but test the spirits to see whether they are from God, because many false prophets have gone out into the world.*

Impatience can be the leader to destruction and causes one to hear another spirit. I start the journey walking with faith as I careful following the inaudible whispering soft whispering voice of the Spirit.

At the Jordan

Once again, the Lord stepped

There are two songs that I sing sometimes: "The Lord will make a way somehow" and "God specializes in things that seem impossible." But the impossible was still impossible. The Lord had yet to make a way somehow for us to return home.

The test wasn't over because there was to be one more test.

The devil knows when we are at our weakest point. I had exhausted all my human efforts to secure a loan. I had gone to almost every bank and lending institution for help and been rejected. I would drive over to Roosevelt Street and look through my spiritual eyes and see our new church building. But then I would look again and see only a hole in the ground ...

Then someone recommended an accountant, a CPA, who offered another way to get the money for our building. I met with him to discuss hiring him to secure a loan for Galatian. He told me that he could promise me a loan. He would "fix" our financial records so they would support the amount that we were trying to borrow.

I was tempted even though I knew it was wrong. I didn't have any other place to go. I told him that I wanted to secure a loan the right way, but that I would go home and give his proposal some thought. At that moment my spiritual ears and eyes were truly open so instead of taking the bait in the power of the Lord's might I decided to wait.

We often say that "God is an on time God" Fortunately, the Lord stepped in just in the nick of time. That same day after I made it made, I received a call from a legitimate mortgage broker. This broker was one the first I talked to in 1994 but told him had secured a loan. Two years later he called and told me that he had spoken to a company that would give us a non-conventional loan.

When we petition God's throne room of grace with our prayer request, we also have to recognize that it is the Lord working things out in our behalf. I didn't care how God did it as long as it got done as long as it was God's way which is the right way.

We finally got the mortgage loan that we so desperately needed. I believe that because the mortgage loan was not a conventional loan, it was just another sign from the Lord to let us know that he was always in control of our situation. While I was giving the Lord praises, my thought was that my faith in the Lord and patience to wait on Him had finally paid off.

Construction on a new building at 5330 Roosevelt Street in Detroit resumed in November 1996.

We had scheduled to march back into our new building on the first Sunday of July the next year 1997 And of course, as Dr. Burroughs had preached, "If it ain't one thing, it is another." The week before our scheduled march-in date, a tornado ripped through the metro-Detroit area. The tornado knocked down trees and power lines in Highland Park, where we had been holding worship services. The tornado had caused major destruction in the city of Detroit which made it difficult to travel on many streets. But on that first

Sunday morning, July 1997 we were determined that nothing was going to stop us from going back home. But something unexpected almost did.

On the Thursday before our march back home on Sunday, I went to the Highland Park building we'd rented on West Grand Street to meet with one of the members of Galatian. It was about 6 p.m., and I was still sitting in my vehicle, parked in the driveway between the church building and a very large tree. It got very dark, almost threatening, and we decided to go inside the building.

About fifteen minutes after we went inside, we heard a noise that sounded like a train. It seemed to last several minutes. We were hearing the tornado cut a path through Highland Park. After the wind died down, we went outside. The large tree that was next to my vehicle had been pulled up and pushed over onto the roof of my vehicle, causing several thousand dollars in damage. Had I been inside, I might not have survived.

Once again, the Lord stepped in right on time and gave us the common sense to go inside before the tornado hit.

Seventh and Final Stop

Victory is mine

The next Sunday, a Detroit police squad, with lights flashing and sirens blasting, came to Highland Park to escort the Galatian caravan safely back home to Roosevelt Street. Mary and I led the way in our car with the rest of the caravan of cars following us through the tornado-hit cities of Highland Park and Detroit. The escort squad led the way drove around knocked-down trees and debris as we made our way back home.

The group that followed Mary and me in the caravan was the same group of loyal and faithful members who had followed Mary and me through the wilderness, who had promised me that they would stick with me through thick and thin. And they did. They all followed Mary and me back home to Roosevelt Street.

When we turned the corner, I looked to my left and gazed upon the beauty of our new church building. Excitement, joy, and tears were all visible on my face. This was our seventh move during our wilderness journey, and the seventh move had brought us back home. Seven represents "completeness."

Horns blowing, we led that loyal and faithful group around several neighborhood blocks, singing that jubilee cry, "Victory is mine. Victory is mine. I told Satan to get thee behind, Victory today is mine."

We then drove into the parking lot. We were all finally home.

To Whom Much Is Given

Being good stewards

I used to wonder about the two years and ten months that we spent wandering through the wilderness. I wondered why the Lord didn't intervene sooner. I never asked from a disrespectful disposition nor from a "Lord, I do not deserve to go through this" mindset. But I did wonder. And here's what I came to believe:

I always believed that there was a lesson the Lord wanted me and the congregation to learn. We as a congregation had allowed the buildings to deteriorate. We were neglectful in keeping up repairs.

As a congregation, we were not good stewards of what the Lord had blessed us with to have and enjoy.

And so I believe the Lord allowed us to go through our wilderness journey to give us time to renew our hearts and minds. I believe the Lord allowed us to go through our wilderness journey so that we would have a greater appreciation for the things He blesses us with. I also believe He wants Galatian and me to learn how to trust Him more in every aspect of our lives.

I remembered that God told Moses that He was the Lord and would deliver Israel from their slavery in Egypt, and they would know that it was God who delivered them and no one else.

I know beyond the shadow of a doubt that it was God's divine intervention that made it possible for us to rebuild back on Roosevelt Street. It was the Lord God who delivered Galatian.

How Can I Forget?

Learning to be thankful

We have been back home on Roosevelt Street for almost fourteen years, and I never miss an opportunity to give praises to whom praises are due. I often remind Galatian, those who were with me during our journey through the wilderness, that the Lord brought us back. We cannot brag about what we have done. We can only be grateful for what the Lord has done for us.

I never miss an opportunity to tell my story to those who joined the Galatian family after we made it back home. I tell them that Galatian and I didn't do anything, but God specializes in things that we thought were impossible. I tell them to look around the edifice, look at the outside of the building—and see what the Lord has done.

During the time that we were wandering through the wilderness after our church was burned down, several churches in the South were set on fire due to racial issues. I know that our situation was the result of a drug dealer who was angry because of our actions to get the drug activity out of the neighborhood. But when funds were sent South to help those churches, Galatian didn't receive any. Although our church had burned down and we needed help, we didn't get any of that help.

But the help we got was far more valuable, and I am most grateful. Two brothers in the Lord who will always have a place in my heart are Pastor Alex Whiteside and Pastor Reginald Caldwell. I don't know what would have become of Galatian had they not opened up their hearts and the doors to their church to me and my Galatian family. I will always be grateful for my extended church family at Antietam Missionary Baptist Church for their love and hospitality.

I am also grateful to three other brothers in the Lord for offering to help us in any way they could. Pastor L. S. Williams, pastor of Goodwill Missionary Baptist Church; Rev. Thomas Cheeks, an associate minister of Goodwill; and the gospel singing group deacon Sam Scott and the Pure Heart Travelers. Deacon Scott is now Pastor Sam Scott.

Pastor Alex Whiteside, who had helped us so much, never got the chance to see our new building. He didn't get the chance to march around the two city blocks and sing with us, "Victory is mine. Victory is mine." But when I look at it from a spiritual perspective, the day the Lord called him home to glory was a victorious day. *Absent from the body ... present with the Lord* (2 Corinthians 5:8).

Pastor Reginald Caldwell and his congregation did come to fellowship and worship with Galatian and with me in our new building. He preached the sermon as we dedicated the building back to the Lord to be used for His purpose. I gave Pastor Caldwell a key to the church building and a key to my office and told him, "My building is your building, my pulpit is your pulpit, and my office is your office."

We were finally back home, where the Lord meant for us to be.

Then in 2006, a pastor and brother in Christ and his congregation found themselves in the same situation that we had been in. They were without a building to worship in. They had nowhere to hold their Bible study and Sunday school.

Just as Galatian and I had moved in with Pastor Alex Whiteside and his congregation, my friend and his congregation moved in with Galatian—for as long as it would take for them to secure a church building.

I told him, "My house is your house, my office is your office, and my pulpit is your pulpit." We shared preaching on Sundays, both choirs sang together, youth ministry worked together, deacons served together, and both congregations worshiped together.

They were with us for four years. Then on the first Sunday in April 2010, my friend and his congregation were blessed to have their first worship service in their own building.

God's blessings continue.

The Lessons

Faith, hope, and patience

There are many lessons I've learned from the many trials and tests of my faith. I learned to trust the Lord more in the midst of spiritual mountains that I may countered. Although there maybe times that I might feel like I am all alone during the journey through life, I am never along. I learned also remember Jesus words to His disciples Matthew 28:20 *Look, I am with you, even until the end of the ages.*

I learned that God can conquer the unconquerable. Faith in Jesus Christ will carry us during the conquest. Faith cannot be measured without testing. Patience is a virtue that only comes from the power of Holy Spirit. Faith and patience are the necessities for hope to live in us as we travel on our Christian journey.

Faith, hope, and patience give believers confidence in knowing that we can withstand life's trials.

Faith, hope, and patience enable every believer in Christ to pass the test.

References

Bibilica, Inc., (1973, 1978, 1984, 2011). **Holy Bible**. Retrieved 03-17-2015, from New International Version & New King James, NIV & NKJV Web Site: Biblegateway.com

II Corinthians 5:8-9 8We are confident, I say, and willing rather to be absent from the body, and to be present with the Lord 9Wherefore we labor, that whether present or absent, we may be accepted of Him.

Matthew 21:21 21Jesus replied, truly I tell you, if you have faith and do not doubt, not only can you do what was done to the fig tree, but also you can say to this mountain, 'Go, throw yourself into the sea, and it will be done.

John 15:18-19 18If the world hates you, keep in mind that it hated Me first 19If you belong to the world, it would love you as its own. As it is, you do not belong to the world, but I have chosen you out of the world. That is why the world hates you.

(Romans 10:9-10 9That if you declare with your mouth, Jesus is Lord," and believe in your heart that God has raised Him from the dead, you will be saved 10For it is with your heart that you believe and are justified, and it is with your and with your mouth that you profess your faith and are saved."

My brethren, count it all joy when ye fall into divers temptations.
—James 1:2

³Because you know that the testing of your faith produces patience
⁴let perseverance have finish it work so that you may be mature and
complete, not lacking anything.
—James 1:3

When tempted by evil, no one should say, God is tempting me, nor
does He tempt anyone.
—James 1:13

Then was Jesus led up of the Spirit into the wilderness, to be tempted
of the devil.
—Matthew 4:1

Psalm 40:-1-3 ¹I waited patiently for the Lord, He turned to me and
heard my cry ²He lifted me out of an slimy pit, out of the mud and
mire and set my feet on a rock and gave me a firm place to stand ³He
has put a new song in my mouth, a hymn of praises unto our God.
Many will see and fear the Lord, and put their trust in Him.

Psalm 121:1-2 ¹I will look up to the hills from where my help comes
²My help comes from the Lord, which made the heavens and the
earth.

2Timothy 2:15 the apostle Paul instructs us to "Study to show
yourself approved, a workman needed not to be ashamed rightly
dividing the word of truth." If you study then you will know who

He, the Holy Spirit is, and how He operates in the lives of believers. Paul also said Faith comes by hearing and hearing the word of God

Romans 10:17. Studying and hearing God's word will keep us and help us patiently wait, while God is working on our behalf.

Acts 9:6 "Lord, here I am, send me" (6:8). And in the words of the apostle Paul: "Lord, what will you have me to do"? (Acts 9:6).

I Peter 5:7-8 [8]Be alert/vigilant and be of sober mind. Your enemy the devil prowls around like a roaring lion looking for someone to devour [9]Resist him, standing firm in the faith, because you know that the family of believers throughout the world is undergoing the same kind of sufferings.

Hebrews 11:1 Now faith is [being sure of] what we hope for and [certain] of what we do not see.
Don't you know that you yourselves are God's temple and that God's Spirit lives in you?

1 Corinthians 3:16: "Don't you know that you yourselves are God's temple and that God's Spirit lives in you?"

Proverbs 3:5–6 teaches us to "Trust in the Lord with all your heart and lean not on your own understanding. In all your ways submit to him, and he will make your paths straight".

Proverbs 16:3-5 [3]Commit to the Lord whatever you do and He will establish you8r plans [4]The Lord works out everything to its proper end. Even the wicked for a day of disaster ⁵The Lord detests all the proud of heart. Be sure of this: they will not go unpunished.

Malachi 3:10 "Bring the whole tithe into the storehouse, that there may be food in my house. Test me in this," says the Lord Almighty, "and see if I will not throw open the floodgates of heaven and pour out so much blessing that there will not be room enough to store it.

Romans 12:1-2, the apostle Paul says ¹Therefore, I urge you, brothers and sisters, in view of God's mercy, to offer your bodies as a living sacrifice, holy and pleasing to God – this your true and proper worship ²Do not conform to the pattern of this world, but be transformed by renewing of your mind. Then you will be able to test and approve what God's will is – His good, pleasing and perfect will.

1 Peter 5:8–9 Be sober, be vigilant; because your adversary the devil walks about like a roaring lion, seeking whom he may devour. Resist him, steadfast in the faith, knowing that the same sufferings are experienced by your [brothers] in the world

Isaiah 41:10 The Lord God is my hope

Psalm 121:1: "I will lift up my eyes to the hills—from where my help comes?"

Matthew 28:20, Jesus promises us: Lo, I am with you always, even unto the end of the world.

James 1:2: "Consider it pure joy … whenever you face trials of many kinds"

Hebrews 11:1 Now faith is substance of things hoped for and the evidence of things not seen."

You have been faithful over a few things, I will make you ruler[s] over many things, 23 NKJV).
Matthew 25:21 How good and how pleasant it is for [brothers] to dwell together in unity!

Proverbs 3:5–6 tells us to Trust in the Lord with all your heart and lean not on your own understanding. In all your ways submit to him, and he will [direct] your path

Psalm 27:1 The Lord is my light and my salvation; whom shall I fear?

Proverbs 3:5 Trust in the Lord with all your heart.

Romans 12:1 The apostle Paul instructed believers to present your bodies [as] a living sacrifice.

II Corinthians 12:7-9 He declares [7]Because of these surpassingly great revelations, therefore, in order to keep me from becoming conceited, I was given a thorn in the flesh. A messenger of Satan, to torment me [8]Three times I pleaded with Lord to take it away (The thorn in the flesh) from me [9]But He said to me, "My grace is sufficient for you, for My power is made perfect in weakness, therefore I will boast all the more gladly about my weakness, so that Christ's power may rest on me.

Galatian 3:3 Are you so foolish? After beginning by means of the Spirit, are you now trying to finish by means of the flesh?

I John 4:1 Dear friends, do not believe every spirit, but test the spirits to see whether they are from God, because many false prophets have gone out into the world.

2 Corinthian 5:8 Absent from the body ... present with the Lord

Matthew 28:20 Look, I am with you, even until the end of the ages.

Printed in the United States
By Bookmasters